Helen KELLER

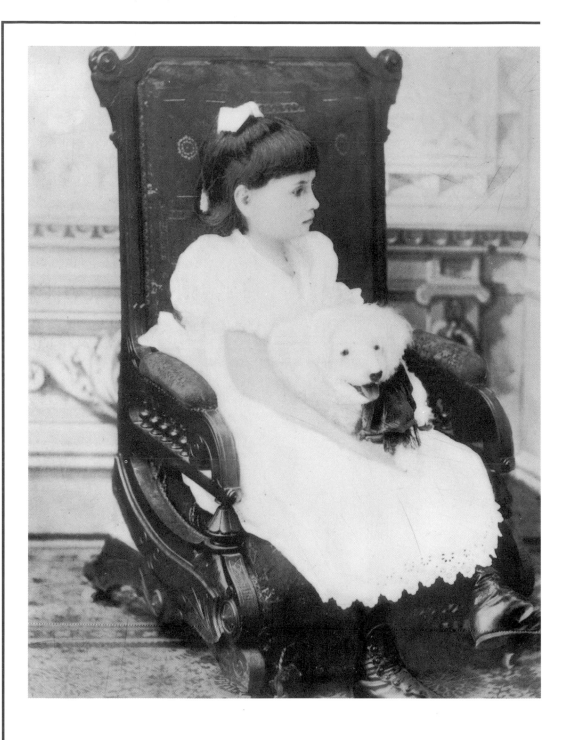

Helen KELLER

Out of a Dark and Silent World

SANDRA H. SHICHTMAN

A Gateway Biography
The Millbrook Press
Brookfield, Connecticut

To Anna Grodzitsky and David and Sylvia Shichtman,
for their love and support

Cover photograph courtesy of the American Foundation for the Blind. Used with permission of the American Foundation of the Blind, Helen Keller Archives.

Photographs courtesy of the American Foundation for the Blind. Used with permission of the American Foundation of the Blind, Helen Keller Archives: pp. 2, 6, 9 (both), 11, 14, 19, 24, 31, 36, 37, 42, 43 (both), 45; AP/Wide World Photos: pp. 16, 39, 41; © Bettmann/Corbis: p. 18; Perkins School for the Blind: p. 21; © Corbis: p. 27; Library of Congress: p. 29; © Hulton-Deutsch Collection/ Corbis: p. 32; Redpath Chautauqua Collection, Special Collections Department, University of Iowa Libraries, Iowa City, Iowa: p. 34

Library of Congress Cataloging-in-Publication Data
Shichtman, Sandra H.
Helen Keller: out of a dark and silent world / Sandra H. Shichtman
p. cm. — (A gateway biography)
Includes index.
Summary: A biography of the deaf and blind woman who overcame her limitations to become a speaker, writer, and advocate for people with disabilities.
ISBN 0-7613-2550-6 (lib. bdg.)
1. Keller, Helen, 1880-1968. 2. Blind-deaf women—United States—Biography—Juvenile literature. [1. Keller, Helen, 1880-1968. 2. Blind. 3. Deaf. 4. Physically handicapped. 5. Women—Biography.] I. Title. II. Series.
HV1624.K4 S55 2002 362.4'1'092—dc21
[B] 2001054650

Published by The Millbrook Press, Inc.
2 Old New Milford Road
Brookfield, Connecticut 06804
www.millbrookpress.com

CONTENTS

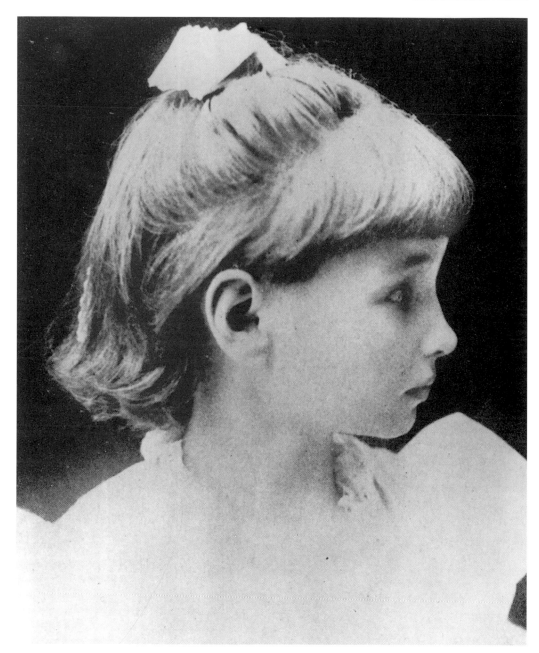

Helen Keller at age six or seven

Introduction Six-year-old Helen Keller was blind and deaf, and she could not speak. She lived in a dark, silent world. But on a warm spring day in 1887, Helen's life changed forever.

All day long Helen could feel that something unusual was going on. Although she could not see or hear, she could feel and smell things better than most people. She could tell that her mother was moving quickly around the house. Her mother's footsteps vibrated on the wooden floor as she rushed from room to room. Her mother's body kicked up a slight breeze as she moved, and Helen could smell her perfume. When Helen reached out her hands and touched her mother's dress, hat, and gloves, the girl knew that Mrs. Keller was going somewhere special.

A puff of air told Helen that her mother had opened the door to go outside. Helen followed her onto the front porch. She wanted to go with her mother, but Mrs. Keller put her hands on Helen's shoulders. Wait here, her hands told Helen. So Helen stayed on the porch step.

She felt her mother get into the carriage. She felt her stepbrother James's heavier footsteps as he got into the carriage, too. The ground shook with the clip-clop of the horse as the carriage rolled away.

Helen's mother and brother were gone for a few hours, but to Helen it seemed that they were away forever. When they finally returned, Helen reached out to hug her mother. But the person she hugged was not her mother. This was a stranger wearing heavy clothing. Helen touched the stranger's clothes, her face, and her hair. Who was this person, she wondered?

Helen would soon find out. This stranger was Anne Sullivan, a young woman the Kellers had hired to be Helen's teacher. Anne would help Helen change from a child who could not see, hear, or speak into a woman who spoke to the world. Years later Helen wrote, "I was caught up and held close in the arms of her who had come to reveal all things to me, and, more than all things else, to love me." But on this day Helen did not know what was in store for her.

A Wild Childhood
Helen Adams Keller was born on June 27, 1880, in Tuscumbia, a small town in northern Alabama. Her father, Arthur Keller, was the editor of a weekly newspaper there. He had fought in the Civil War between the northern and the southern states and become a captain in the Confederate army. Even though the war was over, people still called him "Captain."

Helen's father, Captain Arthur Henley Keller, and Helen's mother, Kate Adams Keller

Kate Keller, Helen's mother, was the Captain's second wife. His first wife had died and left him with two sons, James and Simpson. The boys were almost grown by the time Helen was born.

Helen was Arthur and Kate Keller's first child together. A few years later they had another girl, Mildred, and then a boy, Phillips.

Helen was a happy child, very pretty and very smart. At only six months old, she could say "How d'ye," which meant

"How do you do?" She could say "tea" quite clearly and learned the word "water," which she pronounced "wah wah." And for the first nineteen months of her life, she was a very healthy child.

Then in 1882 she became dangerously ill. She got a high fever that came on very quickly. The Kellers called for a doctor right away. After examining Helen, the doctor shook his head. She had "acute congestion of the stomach and brain," he said. She would probably die.

Doctors today think Helen could have had scarlet fever. People with this illness usually had a very high fever.

Helen didn't die, though, and the high fever went away as suddenly as it had come. But the disease had damaged her eyesight and hearing. In a few weeks she couldn't see or hear anymore. Her world became dark, quiet, and lonely. Before long Helen forgot the words she had learned. She could no longer communicate with anyone.

But a month or two later she began to try to make herself understood by making signs. She nodded when she meant "yes" and shook her head when she meant "no." She pushed to mean "go" and pulled to mean "come." When she wanted bread, she pretended she was cutting a piece of bread and spreading butter on it. If she wanted ice cream, she imitated her mother churning the cream and shivered to show it was cold.

Now Helen's family began to understand her, but they didn't know how to make her understand them. This meant they could not teach her and they had no control over her. Helen began doing whatever she pleased.

Often she did things she knew were wrong. One hot July day in 1886, Helen and Martha Washington, the cook's daughter, were cutting out paper dolls on the front porch. Helen became bored and suddenly used her scissors to snip off some of Martha's hair. Then Martha took the scissors and cut off one of Helen's curls. She was about to cut off another

Young Helen on her porch in Tuscumbia, Alabama

when Mrs. Keller saw what the girls were doing and made them stop.

Another time Helen discovered her baby sister, Mildred, sleeping in her doll's cradle. Angrily, she overturned it. Fortunately, Mrs. Keller caught the baby before she fell to the floor.

And once that same year, when Helen and her mother were alone in the kitchen, Helen locked her mother in the pantry. For three hours Mrs. Keller banged on the pantry door while Helen sat on the porch steps, feeling the vibrations with her hand and laughing.

Something needed to be done with Helen. She was becoming a wild child. Because everyone felt sorry for her, she always got her way and was hardly ever punished for the bad things she did. The family knew this wasn't good for Helen, but what could they do?

Fortunately, Helen's father soon heard of an eye doctor in Baltimore, Maryland, who had helped many blind boys and girls. His name was Dr. Chisholm. Maybe he had the answer.

So Captain Keller took Helen to see Dr. Chisholm. The doctor said he couldn't do anything to help Helen see, but he thought Helen could be educated. He told the Captain about a man in Washington, D.C., who was interested in educating deaf children. That man was Alexander Graham Bell, the inventor of the telephone. Dr. Chisholm said that Mr. Bell could tell Captain Keller what to do for Helen.

On the way back to Tuscumbia, the Captain took Helen to see Mr. Bell. It was a meeting that would change Helen's life.

Mr. Bell thought Helen was a beautiful, delightful child and was very interested in her problem. He told the Captain about the

Perkins Institution for the Blind, a school in Boston that helped both blind and deaf children. He suggested that the Captain write to Michael Anagnos, the head of the school, about Helen.

As soon as Helen and her father got back home, the Captain wrote a letter to Mr. Anagnos, asking him to send someone to Tuscumbia to teach Helen. Mr. Anagnos was happy to help and chose a pretty, dark-haired Perkins student, Anne Sullivan, for the job.

Anne Sullivan came from a very poor family. When her parents died, ten-year-old Anne and her brother were sent to live in the poorhouse in Tewksbury, Massachusetts. When the head of the Board of Charities visited the poorhouse, Anne ran up to him and cried, "I want to go to school." She told him that she couldn't go to school because she was blind. Admiring her spunk, the Board chairman arranged for her to become a student at Perkins in 1880. Anne had two eye operations that restored some of her eyesight, but she would have trouble with her eyes all her life.

Anne Sullivan as a student at Perkins

At Perkins, Anne had learned how to finger-spell words. Finger-spelling is like the sign language that deaf people use. With your fingers, you trace the letters that make up each word into the palm of someone's hand. Mr. Anagnos thought Anne would make a good teacher for Helen.

In those days, people often hired teachers to live in their homes and teach their children.

Early Education Shortly after arriving at the Kellers' house on that warm spring day in 1887, Anne went upstairs to her room to unpack. Helen followed her. Anne gave Helen a doll that the students at the Perkins Institution had sent to her. Helen hugged the doll and began to play with it. While she was playing, Anne took Helen's hand and finger-spelled the letters d-o-l-l into Helen's palm. Helen didn't understand what Anne was doing, but she liked to imitate what other people did. So she spelled d-o-l-l into the air with her fingers, just as Anne had done.

In the weeks that followed, Anne spelled many other words into Helen's hand—"pin," "hat," "cup," "sit," "stand," "walk." Helen imitated what Anne did, but she still had no idea that she was learning words.

Meanwhile, Anne saw that Helen was very wild and had not learned any manners. At mealtimes Helen walked

As Helen got older, she became very good at finger-spelling.

around the table and took food off every-one's plate. She ate with her hands and didn't use her napkin. When Anne asked Captain and Mrs. Keller why they allowed Helen to do that, they said they didn't have the heart to make her behave.

Anne was determined to try. But teaching Helen to sit at the table and eat from her own plate was not easy. Each time Anne tried, Helen resisted. She kept get-ting out of her chair and walking around the table. She kept taking food off everyone's plate with her hands. Finally, Anne slapped Helen's hand when she grabbed some food from Anne's plate. Helen reached out again, and again Anne slapped her hand.

Captain and Mrs. Keller could not bear to watch this. They left the dining room, and Anne locked the door behind them. Now she and Helen were alone and Anne continued the lesson.

Firmly and patiently, Anne picked Helen up and sat her down at the table. Then she picked up Helen's fork and put it into her hand. Helen threw the fork onto the floor. Anne picked the fork up again and gave it back to Helen. Each time Helen got up, Anne carried her back to her chair. Each time Helen threw her fork away, Anne put it back into her hand.

The fight went on for more than an hour, until Helen finally gave up. Now she understood that Anne was in charge. So she sat in her chair, ate her food with a fork, and folded her napkin after the meal.

Captain and Mrs. Keller were surprised and pleased to see their wild child sitting quietly at the table. Anne was pleased, too, but also very tired.

Anne told the Kellers that she could do a better job of teaching Helen if they could live by themselves for a while. The Kellers agreed. The Kellers' home was on a plantation called Ivy Green. Near the main house was a smaller cottage. For two weeks Anne and Helen lived there alone together. During that time Anne helped Helen dress, comb her hair, and bathe. She also played games with her and taught her how to string beads and crochet. And every day, she spelled more words into Helen's hand.

The water pump where Helen learned to finger-spell her first word—"water"

One day Anne took Helen to the water pump in the yard. Anne pumped the handle up and down. She put Helen's hand under the spout and held it there. Water flowed from the spout while Anne spelled w-a-t-e-r into Helen's hand. She poured out some more water and spelled w-a-t-e-r again and then again into Helen's hand. Finally, Helen's face lit up with understanding. She remembered that she had learned to say "wah wah" for "water" when she was a baby. Now she knew that there was a word for everything and that Anne could teach her to finger-spell those words.

Helen wanted to know more words. She touched everything she could reach and demanded to know the word for it. Anne followed her, holding her hand and spelling each word into it. Learning quickly, Helen spelled the words back into Anne's hand. She learned "mother," "father," "sister," "teacher," and many other words that day. And from that day on, Teacher was the name she always called Anne.

After Helen and Anne returned to the main house, Anne taught Helen's family how to finger-spell, too. Now everyone could talk to Helen and she could talk to them. Anne Sullivan had brought Helen Keller out of her lonely world.

That summer Anne also taught Helen to read special books that Anne had brought from the Perkins Institution.

Helen demonstrates the manual alphabet.

One-Hand Manual Alphabet

The One-Hand Manual Alphabet is spelled through the touch of fingers into the palm of the blind person's hand; it differs very slightly from the sign-language alphabet of deaf people who cannot speak.

The invention of the manual alphabet is attributed to Spanish monks, living under a vow of silence, in medieval times. First standardized and officially adopted in France in the 18th century for the education of hearing and speech impaired persons, it was later adapted for deaf-blind persons by British and American educators.

Helen Keller learned to use this alphabet—illustrated here in photographs of her hands—when she was six and a half years old. She was deaf, blind, and had almost no form of communication when Anne Sullivan came to teach her. One month after Anne Sullivan began spelling into her palm, Helen showed her association of the alphabet with the world around her when she recognized her first word: "Water."

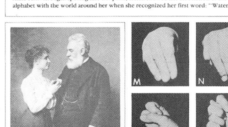

The photograph shows Helen Keller speaking to Alexander Graham Bell by means of the manual alphabet when she was a 22-year-old student at Radcliffe.
The photo is by Marshall, Boston, 1902.

These special books had pages of heavy paper with raised print. By feeling the print with her fingers, Helen quickly learned to make out the letters and words. She soon read all the books Anne had brought, so Anne wrote to Mr. Anagnos for more books. Mr. Anagnos sent more raised-print books as well as some special books that the teachers at Perkins had made. The words in these special books were formed from raised dots instead of raised letters. This kind of writing is called braille.

Braille was invented by a blind Frenchman named Louis Braille. Each group of dots spells a letter of the alphabet. The dots are made by pushing up the paper on one side of the page and then turning the page over. Blind people touch the raised dots with their fingers in order to read the words.

Within six months Anne was again running out of books for her student. She asked the Kellers if she could take Helen to Perkins. There would be many more books at Perkins for Helen to read, she said, and Helen could also learn mathematics, history, and geography there. The Kellers agreed that Helen should go, and, in May 1888, Mrs. Keller took Helen and Anne to the school.

The children at Perkins welcomed Helen to their school. Like her, they knew how to finger-spell. Helen later wrote, "What joy to talk with other children in my own language!"

Before long, Helen was happily talking and playing with the other children. She learned to play the piano, keeping the rhythm by feeling the vibrations of the piano keys. She learned to work with her hands, doing beadwork, knitting, and clay modeling.

She also learned to read and write French and Greek. Helen wrote with a pencil on a sheet of paper placed over a board with deep grooves across it. Her left hand guided her right hand, so that she could write between the grooved lines. Anne taught Helen some subjects, and other teachers taught her as well.

Sometimes Anne and Mrs. Keller took Helen to interesting places around Boston that she had read

At Perkins, eleven-year-old Helen (top left) met other deaf and blind students.

about in her history books. They took her to visit Bunker Hill, where American colonists fought for their freedom from England. They took her to Plymouth, where the Pilgrims landed in 1620. Helen touched Plymouth Rock. Later she wrote that this excited her imagination. She thought the Pilgrims were very brave to have left their homes to come to a strange new land.

That summer Anne and Mrs. Keller took Helen to Cape Cod, a peninsula in Massachusetts with beautiful beaches. Helen had never been to the ocean before. She waded out into the water. When the waves knocked her over, she got some water in her mouth. "Who put salt in the water?" she finger-spelled into Anne's hand when she was safely back on dry land. Anne thought that was funny.

At that time children who were blind and deaf did not go to school. Most of them never learned to read and write.

At the end of the summer, Mrs. Keller went home to Tuscumbia and Helen and Anne returned to the Perkins Institution. Mr. Anagnos and Helen's other teachers were amazed that Helen had learned to read and write so well. She was the only child at Perkins who was both blind and deaf.

Mr. Anagnos asked Anne to write an article explaining how she taught Helen. He published the article in the school's year-end report. Many wealthy people who gave money to help run the school read the report with great interest. They and others wanted to know more about Helen's remarkable achievements and how Anne taught her. Newspaper reporters also wrote stories about Helen and Anne. Student and teacher were becoming famous.

A New Language In 1890 one of the teachers at the Perkins Institution returned from a trip to Norway with some amazing news. There she had met another blind and deaf girl, Ragnhild Kaata. Like Helen, this girl had learned to read and write. But she had also learned to speak. As soon as Helen heard the story, she decided that she wanted to learn to speak, too.

Everyone at Perkins told her that it would be very hard for her to speak. How can you speak a word without first hearing it? they asked. But Helen decided that if Ragnhild Kaata could speak, she could do it, too. She kept asking Anne to find someone to teach her. Finally, Anne heard about the Horace Mann School in Boston, where deaf children were learning to speak.

With the Kellers' permission, Anne took Helen to the Horace Mann School in March 1890. When Sarah Fuller, the principal of the school, met Helen, she was so moved by Helen's eagerness to learn that she promised to teach Helen herself.

The first lesson started with Sarah placing Helen's fingers on Sarah's tongue and lips. Helen felt the teacher's

Helen reads lips with her fingers.

tongue and lips and the puff of air when she made a sound. Then Helen imitated her teacher with her own tongue and lips. At the end of the first lesson, Helen could make the sounds for M, P, A, S, T, and I. She had ten more lessons after that. The first sentence Helen spoke was "I am warm."

When the lessons were finished, Helen and Anne went home to Tuscumbia. "I am not dumb now," Helen told her family happily. It was hard to understand Helen when she spoke. Her voice sounded as if she couldn't breathe through her nose—not like the voice of someone who can hear. But that did not matter to Helen. She could speak and that made her very happy.

A Dream of College When she was just a little girl, Helen told her family and friends, "Some day I shall go to college. I shall go to Harvard." But only men could go to Harvard at that time. When Helen learned this, she declared that she would go to Radcliffe instead, a prestigious college for young women near Harvard.

Many people told Helen that studying at Radcliffe was very difficult for young women who could see and hear and speak. It would be nearly impossible for someone who could not. Even Radcliffe's dean, Agnes Irwin, told her to choose another college. But Helen was determined to become a student at Radcliffe. Only Anne knew it would be useless to try to change Helen's mind.

Helen understood that to go to Radcliffe she would have to pass a difficult entrance examination. She also knew she would have to learn to speak better. She asked her father for speech lessons, but he said he didn't have the money to pay for them. She would have to find another way to pay for the lessons, or her dreams of going to college would never come true. Fortunately, a rich and charitable man from Boston, John P. Spaulding, heard about Helen's plans and gave her the money.

With Anne by her side, Helen, now fourteen, left for the Wright-Humason School for the Deaf in New York City in the fall of 1894. It was considered the best school in the country for teaching deaf children how to speak. In her two years at Wright-Humason, Helen learned to speak English more clearly. She also took lessons in French and German. She met many rich and famous people in New York who were impressed with her and wanted to help pay for her education.

Now Helen had enough money to go to a school that would further prepare her for Radcliffe. She chose the Cambridge School for Girls in Cambridge, Massachusetts. There she studied English history and literature, German, Latin, and arithmetic. She made friends with girls of her own age who could see and hear and speak. Every day Anne sat next to her in her classes and spelled all the lessons into her hand. Helen's friends translated the books she needed into braille and raised print so she could read them herself.

Things were going very well for Helen, but in August 1896 she got the sad news that her father had died. Helen desperately wanted to go home for the funeral, but she had to stay at school to finish her studies. However, as soon as school was out for the summer, Helen went back to Tuscumbia to be with her family.

It took Helen three more years of study, first at Cambridge School and then with a tutor, before she was ready to take the col-

While at Radcliffe, Anne read Helen's lessons to her.

lege entrance examination in June 1899. She shocked many people at Radcliffe, especially Agnes Irwin, by passing the test. Then, in the fall of 1900, Helen began her first year at Radcliffe. Anne, of course, went with her.

Work at college is hard even for students who can see and hear, but it was even harder for Helen because she couldn't.

Still, Helen did very well at Radcliffe. Anne sat beside Helen in her classes and spelled what the teachers said into her hand. Very few of the books Helen needed were written in braille or raised print, so Anne also spent many hours spelling the words from the books into Helen's hand.

During Helen's second year at Radcliffe, an editor at the *Ladies' Home Journal* magazine asked her to write a series of articles about her life. He thought his readers would be interested in knowing how Helen learned to read and write, what she learned in the schools she went to, what places she visited, and what people she met along the way. Although Helen was very busy with college work, she decided to write the articles anyway.

Helen needed someone to help her, but Anne wasn't able to do much because her eyes were getting weaker and weaker. So Helen hired a Harvard English teacher, John Albert Macy, to help her write and edit her articles. John quickly learned how to finger-spell so he could talk to Helen.

People loved Helen's articles because they told of a life very different from theirs. The articles were printed as a book in 1903. The book, which was called *The Story of My Life*, became very popular and is still sold in bookstores today.

Helen graduated from Radcliffe in 1904 with honors. Since Helen was the first blind and deaf person ever to earn a college degree, many newspaper reporters wrote articles about her achievement. Helen was happy because she had proven that a deaf and blind person could succeed in col-

Helen graduated from Radcliffe in 1904,
when she was twenty-four years old.

lege. Years later, when President Woodrow Wilson asked Helen why she went to Radcliffe, she told him, "Because they didn't want me at Radcliffe."

Speaker, Writer, Crusader

When Helen graduated from Radcliffe in 1904, she bought an old farmhouse in Wrentham, Massachusetts, with the money she had earned from her book. Anne moved in with her and John was a constant visitor. During this time Anne and John fell in love, and in 1905 they got married. After the honeymoon, the couple returned to Wrentham to live with Helen.

Now the three lived as a family. John strung wires around the property so Helen could go for walks by herself, holding on to the wires so she would not get lost. They played chess, discussed the events of the day, entertained their many friends, and made plans for their future.

Helen knew she must earn her own living, but she wasn't quite sure what her life's work was going to be. She knew she wanted to help blind people, and she knew she wanted to write. So when the editor of *Century* magazine asked her to write some essays about how she learned about the world around her, Helen was happy to do it. As he had before, John helped her write and edit her essays. This time, Anne was well enough to help Helen, too.

Helen wrote that she learned much through smelling— she said that she could smell a storm coming and that each

Helen, Anne, and John on the porch at Wrentham

house had its own separate smell. She also wrote that she learned by touching things. "My hand is to me what your hearing and sight together are to you," she said in one essay. "It is the hand that binds me to the world of men and women."

In 1908 the essays were printed as a book called *The World I Live In*. Like her first book, this one became very popular. People were still interested in hearing about Helen because her life was so different from theirs.

Being blind and deaf could not keep Helen from writing throughout her life.

Helen would write a number of other books in her lifetime and dozens of magazine and newspaper articles. She wrote about issues that she was deeply concerned about—religion, women's and workers' issues, war, and the living conditions of the poor.

But writing wasn't enough for Helen. First, it didn't bring in enough money. Second, she wanted to be more active in working for blind people and in convincing others that blind people could learn. She also wanted to do more for the other causes she believed in. But what should she do? After much thought, she and Anne decided to plan a speaking tour. Already Helen had given several speeches.

Helen had been working with the American Association of Workers for the Blind, a group of people who wanted blind adults to go to school and to work. Most blind children didn't go to school in those days, so they couldn't work when they grew up. Helen had once given a speech to a group of state leaders in Massachusetts, asking them to find a way for blind adults to learn how to make things they could sell.

Now, to prepare for the speaking tour, Helen again took voice lessons to improve her speech. Then, in 1913, Helen and Anne made their first public appearance in New Jersey. First Anne spoke, telling how she had turned a wild young girl into a wonderful young woman who could read and write.

Because of Anne's illness, Helen hired Peter Fagan to help her. Soon Helen and Peter fell in love and wanted to get married, but Mrs. Keller did not approve and sent Peter away. Helen never got married.

Next Helen said that every blind and deaf person could be educated just as she had been. Finally, Helen answered questions from the audience. The speaking tour made many more people interested in helping blind children and adults.

After two months on the tour, Anne became ill and the two women had to return to Wrentham. But there would be many more speeches. After Anne recovered, in 1914, they set off on a tour of eastern cities. Then they gave speeches all

THE MOST REMARKABLE LECTURE EVER GIVEN

HELEN KELLER

And her Teacher **Mrs. Macy** (Anne M. Sullivan)

MISS KELLER'S SUBJECT WILL BE

"HAPPINESS" Preceded by the story of her life, by Mrs. Anne S. Macy

A circular announces Helen and Anne's lecture series.

over the United States and Canada. This time they took with them Polly Thomson, a young woman from Scotland whom they hired as an assistant and secretary. John was no longer living with Anne and Helen, but he and Anne never divorced.

During her lifetime Helen gave hundreds of speeches. She spoke out for blind and deaf people. She spoke out for women, workers, and the poor. She spoke out against war. In one speech in New York City, Helen told the people, "I look upon the world as my Fatherland, and every war has for me the horror of a family feud."

The lectures were very successful. They changed how people thought about women, workers, the poor, and war. They also caused people to give thousands of dollars to organizations to help blind and deaf people.

Actor and Entertainer
In 1918 Helen and Anne got an interesting proposal. Dr. Francis Trevelyan Miller, a writer, said that he wanted to write a movie about Helen's life. The movie would be called *Deliverance* and it would show how Anne Sullivan had saved Helen from the dark, quiet world of the blind and deaf. He wanted Helen to play herself.

Helen thought a movie would earn her a lot of money and she accepted. She, Anne, and Polly went to Hollywood so Helen could become an actress.

The man who directed the movie was George Foster Platt. He told Anne what he wanted Helen to do and Anne

A scene from Deliverance, *a movie about Helen's life*

finger-spelled what he said into Helen's hand. He also
tapped on the floor when he wanted Helen to walk. Helen
could feel the taps with her feet and moved as soon as she
felt them. Three taps might mean "walk forward three
steps." Another tap might mean "sit in the chair."

Unfortunately, the movie was a flop. People liked action
movies and love stories, and the movie about Helen didn't
have either. Helen was disappointed at the small amount of
money she earned from the movie.

But in 1920 Helen and Anne found a way to earn a lot of money. They joined a vaudeville show, a variety show with acrobats, animals, and a bird act. Helen and Anne had their own act in the show.

The act that Helen and Anne did was very different from the others in the show. First Anne came out onto the stage and talked about how she taught Helen to read, write, and speak with her fingers. Then Helen finger-spelled and spoke for a few minutes. Finally, people in the audience asked Helen some questions. A popular question was "How can you dream if you can't see?" Because people everywhere were interested in Helen's story, it was one of the most popular acts in the show.

Helen and Anne do their vaudeville act around 1920.

Many of Helen's friends and family were horrified about her new vaudeville career. Lecturing was dignified, they thought, but vaudeville was low-class. But Helen liked being in vaudeville and it solved her money problems. The audiences loved her, and she earned more money in vaudeville than she got from writing books or from giving speeches. So she and Anne stayed in the show for two years.

In June 1921, while Helen and Anne were on tour in Los Angeles, Mrs. Keller died. Helen got the news just two hours before she had to go on the stage. She was very upset, and she didn't think she could do her act. But she also knew that people had paid money to see and hear her, and she felt she owed it to them to perform. So she stopped crying, walked onto the stage, and did her part of the act. It was probably Helen's greatest performance as an actor.

Raising Money for the Blind By now Helen was one of the most famous women in the world. But money was still a problem for her, Anne, and Polly. They had to give up their house in Wrentham and move into a smaller one in Forest Hills, New York. Soon, however, some of their wealthy friends set up a fund to provide money for their future expenses. Free from money worries for the first time, the three women continued to work tirelessly for the causes they believed in.

In 1923 Helen and Anne were asked to raise money for the American Foundation for the Blind. This national organization was started in 1921 by people who wanted to give blind and deaf/blind people the same chance to go to school and work as people who could see. Helen and Anne agreed to help. In a speech she gave in Brooklyn, New York, Helen said, "A national service dedicated to the deaf/blind is essential, and I pledge myself to do whatever I can for its accomplishment."

Between 1923 and 1926 they spoke to 250,000 people in 123 cities across the country. They went to lunches and dinners and parties to talk to people

Helen with her dog in New York City in 1939

who gave thousands of dollars to help the American Foundation for the Blind do its work. Between 1930 and 1933 they sailed to Europe to help workers for the blind raise money for blind people there. They also visited children in schools for the blind and blind patients in hospitals.

But all this travel was hard on Anne. By now she was nearly seventy and almost blind herself, and her health was getting worse. She was tired all the time and needed to rest. So Helen stopped traveling and stayed at home, hoping her old teacher would get better. But that didn't happen. Anne Sullivan died in October 1936. Her ashes were placed in the National Cathedral in Washington, D.C.

To honor Anne Sullivan, Helen called her new house Arcan Ridge, after a town in Scotland they had visited together. When Arcan Ridge burned down in 1947, friends gave Helen money to rebuild it.

Her teacher's death made Helen feel as though she had lost a part of herself. She wondered how she could go on without Anne, who had been at her side for almost fifty years. But she also knew there was still much work to do for the blind.

So after Anne's death, Helen and Polly began traveling again, raising more money for blind people in Europe and Asia and visiting schools and hospitals there. They returned home in 1938 and moved to quiet Westport, Connecticut.

*At her Westport, Connecticut, home, Helen had railings
built so she could take walks on her own.*

World War II started in 1939, putting an end to Helen's
overseas travels. When the United States entered the war in
1941, President Franklin Delano Roosevelt asked Helen to
visit American hospitals and talk to injured soldiers and

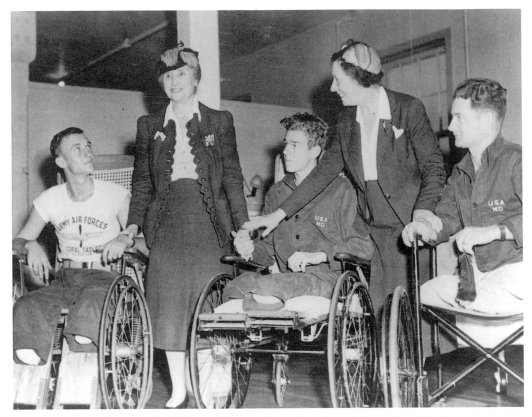

Helen and Polly talk with injured soldiers in 1944.

sailors there. Helen explained to blind soldiers that blind-
ness was not the end of the world. They could still walk and
read, she said, but they would now walk with a cane and
read with their fingers. She told deaf sailors that they could
hear with their eyes. Her visits gave courage and hope to
everyone who met her. After all, they thought, she never let
being blind and deaf keep her from doing anything she
wanted.

Once the war ended in 1945, Helen and Polly resumed their world travels, again raising money for schools and work opportunities for blind people all over the world. Between the years 1945 and 1957 they visited schools and hospitals in thirty-five different countries.

Helen meets with a blind South African and his child in 1950.

Helen and Polly on a visit to Japan

A Shining Light Helen and Polly continued their travels, raising money and bringing hope to the blind. But in 1957 Polly had a stroke, which is caused by a blood clot in the brain. She never got better and died in 1960. Her ashes were placed next to Anne's in the National Cathedral in Washington, D.C.

Helen was eighty years old when Polly died. Without her dear friend by her side, she decided it was time to stop traveling. She went back to Arcan Ridge. There, she spent the last years of her life reading, writing letters, and visiting with friends who came from all over the world to see her.

Throughout her life, Helen had received many honors for her work in helping blind and deaf people. On June 2, 1965, she got one more honor. The U.S. Senate passed a resolution in her honor. It said that "in recognition of the vast contributions made by Miss Helen Keller to the well-being of all humanity, the Senate extends its greeting and best wishes to Miss Keller on her eighty-fifth birthday."

Helen Keller died on June 1, 1968, just before her eighty-eighth birthday. Her ashes were placed beside Anne's and Polly's in the National Cathedral in Washington, D.C.

People all over the world were saddened by Helen's death. Letters and telegrams poured in from presidents, kings, and queens she had known and from ordinary people who had never met her. Now they all wanted to say thank you to the woman who had overcome her own disabilities and become a tireless crusader for blind people all over the world.

Helen at age eighty reads a book written in braille.

IMPORTANT DATES

1880	Helen Keller is born on June 27 in Tuscumbia, Alabama.
1882	Helen loses her sight and hearing.
1887	Anne Sullivan comes to Tuscumbia on March 3 to teach Helen.
1900	Helen becomes a student at Radcliffe College.
1902	Helen writes magazine articles for the *Ladies' Home Journal*. They are published the next year as a book called *The Story of My Life*.
1904	Helen graduates from Radcliffe College.
1908	Helen's second book, *The World I Live In*, is published.
1913–1916	Helen and Anne tell people all over the country how Helen learned to read, write, and talk. Helen hires Polly Thomson to be her secretary.
1918	Helen stars in a movie about her life.
1930–1933	Helen, Anne, and Polly travel in Europe to raise money to help blind people there.
1936	Anne Sullivan dies in October.
1945–1957	Helen and Polly visit blind and deaf people in many countries.
1960	Polly dies.
1968	Helen Keller dies on June 1.

INDEX

About the Author   Sandra H. Shichtman is a former English teacher and textbook editor. She frequently writes for and about people with disabilities. Her articles and stories have appeared in many national children's and adult magazines. She and her husband, Michael, live in New York City near their son, Mark, and their daughter-in-law, Joan.